Call Waiting

David C. Ward is Senior Historian at the National Portrait Gallery, Smithsonian Institution, where he has curated exhibitions including *Hide/Seek: Difference and Desire in American Portraiture* (2010) and *Poetic Likeness: Modern American Poets* (2012). He is also the author of *Charles Willson Peale: Art and Selfhood in the Early Republic* (2004). He holds graduate degrees from the University of Warwick and Yale University. His short collection of poems, *Internal Difference*, was published by Lintott/Carcanet in 2011.

DAVID C. WARD

Call Waiting

CARCANET

First published in Great Britain in 2014 by
Carcanet Press Limited
Alliance House
Cross Street
Manchester M2 7AQ

www.carcanet.co.uk

A CIP catalogue record for this book is available from the British Library

ISBN 978 1 84777 226 8

The publisher acknowledges financial assistance from Arts Council England

Typeset by XL Publishing Services, Exmouth
Printed and bound in England by SRP Ltd, Exeter

In Memory
of
My Parents

I never could figure you guys out…

Harvest is past, summer is ended, and we are not saved.

– Jeremiah 8:20

Contents

I

II

III

I

June, Swoon

Insomniacs know
The indifferent moon
Cares naught for you.

But it's always there
Just when you need it,
The tidal pull

At blood and heart –
A white page, a canvas.
My pencil. Start.

River Run

Sure why not? It's not like the river banks
Are any closer after all these years. But even we
Were surprised when the bridge packed up and left
For parts unknown.
Search parties were noncommittal and the trees looked askance
When asked about the circumstances.
The river hardly noticed but then it wouldn't, would it?
Could be worse of course.
But that's what they always say

Those wiseacres down at City Hall with their fancy
Ways and spats. Still the light still comes up
Shyly delivering the news and all its portents.
My, how the town has grown!
The buildings all so tall.
So blue.

Slake

Rest on your haunches
At stream-side.
Cup your hands together.
Bow toward the further bank.
Balanced, dip your hands;
Let the water fill
The bowl of your hands;
Raise them from the water.

Drink from your bowled hands.
Bowing, drink again from the cup
You hold in your hands.
Rising, cup your face
In your cooled hands.

Think of where
You have to go today.
Go there.

Debridement

Simplify, simplify.
Debride the wounds that life inflicts:
Sluice out the debris and corrupt skin
That infects the body and the world.
Pick out the poisoned fabric shards
And heal yourself naked and whole again
In cold springs among high mountain pines.
Give yourself over to something other
Than yourself and let your body fall free
In clouds of lavender that raise you up
To live reborn and on your terms:
Simplify, simplify.
Embrace, embrace.

The Absolute Sweetness of Decay

Fragrancing ancient orchards
Musky smell of fallen apples,
Beauty of tumbled farmsteads, broken walls
And sprawl of meadows hazed by late autumn
Heat – winter's coming on.

Learn from this. Divest yourself of illusions
Of control. Beware of plans: plans fail.
Do the wrong thing, well.
And when you die, scatter your ashes
High into the electric air.

Still we pretend at modesty

These days, dreams of modest heroism
cloud even the smallest tyrant's mind.
Who is exempt from self-effacing grandeur?
No one is an erratic driver or a bad lover
when history is behind the wheel of fate.
We can't kid ourselves: we all acquiesce.
Everything is in play now, even quiet
moments down by the old mill pond
are a product placement opportunity.
But still we play at modesty even as we rise
like trout to plaudits which sting our mouths
with ashes of electronic funds. Rinse, repeat:
was any complex civilization ever founded
on such a simple formulation?

                So Katy, bar the door,
and if you're doing nothing tonight, please drop by?
We'll each keep a foot on the floor, like pool players,
and keep company for a while. You won't stay.
Who does these days? One (notice the distancing
pronoun) gets used to it. Yet alone or not, sometimes
in the waking dream of night, cutting the electronic
clutter that now hums our synapses, I smell white water
and follow the tracery of rivers among cold pines.

No Place

With no more news from nowhere
it's hard to fathom any more.
Nostalgia's a frail reed to justify
lives lived to the rhythm of TV dinners
and traffic reports. The verities of
weather trouble us only on video while
our lives seal us up with air-borne mites
and molds. Where did all these lung
ailments come from anyway? The pine-
scented fresheners don't work and
wearied by the ersatz sublime desperate
measures are required, at least by some.

Poor heart: no more Aeolian string humming the
hyperbolic ether, a dynamo gorgeously
electrifying us in all our struggles and up against
which we were fierce in losing. Now the thrum is
all inside while our internal air crusts up channels,
rimes tear ducts shut with salt. A recurring dream
keeps breaking into halcyon day nights of sleep:
a river shimmers just beyond that near-distant line of trees.
So close, we could almost walk there if we would.

Self-Reliance

In the books, old-time private eyes
Worked alone, keeping to a solitary code.
These days, the 'eye'
Has a sidekick who reads the signs,
Watches his back and kills the someone
Who needs killing
When the hero scruples. He's always laconically
Amused, ready with a quip after the showdown
Cordite clears – justice balanced out.

I've discovered
Life's nothing like it says in books:
You have to do the dirty work yourself.

Any Questions?

Just between you, me and the electronic ether,
Doesn't everything these days seem out of kilter?
Streets are out of tune and every passing car
Shifts the axis further out of true. Buildings sway
Slightly in the light but their shadows end up always
Somehow 'off' in ways that are perplexing. Days slide
By unnoticed, anniversaries come and go
Like blank pages in my diary. Time's up!

Meanwhile, remote ice floes following clouds
Chip their way south, sea birds wheel
To a rhythm we can't fathom. Time to go,
Going someplace else. I think a boat
Leaves at 10 o'clock tonight. I'm on it.

Another Birthday

Curiously enough, experience was a hard master
but like likes like and things evened out
in the end. Subway cars rattled past
on opposite tracks while the whoosh of air
left coattails flying. If your destination is the park,
Madam, you're going the wrong way. But perhaps
you'll get there anyway – things balance out keeping
things from becoming too fraught.

We've learned to ride our luck.
Word on the street is that summer will be late
this year but meteorologically speaking,
what's the difference? Buildings keep getting taller,
elevators faster, and all the while the murmur of
distanced voices remind us of the missing.

These Days

So that's all right then, the ends do justify
The beginnings, but it's hard to know where we stand
Right now. Smoke rings are *verboten*
But advertisements have a pornographic allure
As if airbrushed clean of avarice. 'The thing in itself'?
I don't think so. Only a philosopher would know for sure.
Boy howdy! I sure don't. But that's to be expected:
These years childhood doesn't prepare us much

For understanding anything. Youthful promise
Fades fast these days against the tarnishing of all that glitz
And chrome. Eternal verities, indeed,
Turn out not to be so long-lasting in the end.
You might as well start over for all you've learned.
Another false start, another clock ringing somewhere else.

Anything special

going on? Me neither so set a spell.
No need to say anything, just enjoy the view,
it always changes without ever seeming to.
A trick of the light perhaps, so the painters said.
I have my doubts.
Why doesn't matter dematerialize
before our very eyes? Should we really trust
our senses to something so important?
Anyway, I like the idea of far-off vistas
floating away like clouds, trees becoming less
than whole, branches and leaves quietly
exploding, the trunk unsolid
in the wavering air. Why think the whole
is merely the sum of its parts? Look closer.

Pole Star

Perhaps you didn't hear me correctly:
the moss grows always on the north side
of trees. *And so the trackless wilderness extends*
endless into space leaving us bereft of any
sense of where we are. Delirium...
Leaving home is disorienting enough
without forgetting the lexicon of woodlore
assembled by our ancestors and left for us
to follow. Credulous, we believe only in ourselves,
paying the price in false starts or voyages
to places we didn't want to go. Make the best of it!
But above all, remember what you've learned
from those who've gone before. The principles
are easy enough to follow if you're of a mind.

Say again? I didn't catch that

No, I distinctly remember putting the payment in the mailbox
Down the end of the street. It was a gray day, the sun
                                        came out later,
When the waitress arrived with refreshments. Not that day –
The other one. You know the one I mean: when the
                                        streets disappeared
Somewhere out in country fields and all connections were cut off.
Kind of nice really, the sense of calm – the quiet that is the cliché
Of evenings passing through the entire day. The *something*
Hush of *something* sacrifice – something like that anyway.
You know what I mean. It will come to me.

Later on, of course, the circuits
Sparked on line again and generators thrummed back into life.
The life we know anyway, the one we've grown familiar in.
Funny to think of how it was before. Hills, the line of trees
Picked out against the blue-black dawn-lit sky, the Morning Star –
The sense of falling into fresh-mown meadows: so fast, so far.

Time and Tide

Maybe there's nothing to it
but the moon does exert its tidal pull
even on crowded streets.
People look upwards and then hurry off
to sites unseen, appointments half-
remembered. There's a point to all this
I think but meaning is obscure
when all you carry is a compass
along with your vague aspiration to end up
somewhere else. Someplace safe?
Or just someplace different from where
you started. Streams quicken at their source
but meander with time and distance.
Lucky old moon, pushing things along.

Berkshire Spring, False Dawn

That spring we resolved to wait, not to be fooled
By early warmings, the melt of the ice and snow.
We resisted ecstasy, avoided the Dionysian tendency,
Looked askance at all temptations promised by a joyful
Sense of new beginnings. We knew the Puritan divines,
Our forebears, had always gotten nature right:
Graveyard of hope – trust only in the severity of God
And what He has in store for us – playthings in His hands.

Still… the hesitant appearance of green shoots along the roads
Upthrust through grimy ice, the trickle flow of meltwater
Down the mountain to swell the streams and river washed
Our best resolved intentions away. Our veins pulsed
Faster with the promise of annual renewal.
The result was swift: Easter blizzard, two feet on the ground.

Climate Change

After the War, everyone bought cars and traffic jams moved
West, along roads flung out willy-nilly across the rolling
Hills of what was once prairie land. Jimcrackery flourished
And neon lights burned out the stars. The moon lingered
Watchfully on the horizon and frequently fell from view,
Thinking things over for a while. In sudden wind
Hats blew off and vanished for good. People felt more comfortable
In groups, especially in movie houses which saw a boom
In double bills and popped corn. Double-sealed window glass
And air conditioning created the climate of the future – now!
Everything was affordable and even possible with just a small
Down payment, made today. A minority kept a wary eye
Out for changes but weather forecasts were, as always, mixed.
Those 'in the know' promised things would never change
As the rivers overflowed and geese flew south in June.

'Warning! Cliff Edge! Danger!!'

I see you have no fear of heights. Not me,
I've never been one for the high escarpment,
The windy bluff overlooking… nothing at all
Except the temptation to let go, and fall
Spinning into what's unknown, drawn on by the air.
Better to keep quiet, risk nothing, stay
Close held, at home. Or else why say
That home is where you hang your heart?
Proverbs are a useful guide, I've found, to safe

Conduct through life's risky crossings.
Read the paper by the fire, venture nothing, gain
Nothing. Where's loss? Nothing but a life –
The one thing we can all afford to lose.
The pathway's clearly marked! Don't stray too far!

Drowning Narcissus

No, you're not in any especial danger.
Know you're not the center of the pool.
Realize that the blue-gold blueness of the sky
is always racing indifferently away,
uncaring of whatever you're up to today
or any other day. Tear your gaze away
and follow on. Consider the orange.
Avoid old ventures requiring new shoes.
Learn how to shrug – eloquently –
while watching where you walk, not how.
But use a plumb bob to fix your posture
and since fecklessness is the other side
of the old coin, keep a weather eye.
For good luck, tattoo a hex sign over
your heart. But above all else, cut
the chatter, especially to yourself.
Prune vigorously, blending a new masque
from last year's gleanings. Cultivate
a different diction but don't expect results
in less than a lifetime. So take time
to fallow for a little while or a while longer.
Flow your sense of touch over the world's skin.
Unstop your years. Try listening
through your eyes and turn down the light
level of the noise. Consider yourself as
a net that gives back its takings –
know which is which and stay off the median.
Separate your body from yourself,
like skin from fruit from pith from zest.

Peel the orange.

Chancellorsville

I'd like to have an audacious idea
Every once in a while:
Shake things out and act
On a bare glimmer traced
Through the brambled underbrush
Discern the patterns
Read the signs, see the crows
Crosshatched against the sky
Fluttering south, away from something
Out there, just *there*, see it?
Riding into wilderness, cutting ties
Leaving everything behind
The air closing as I pass
Inviolate into the future
Set the rabbits running
Down the road and following
With a clear sense
Only of the now, the ever present
Moment sealing off the past
Only the future on the horizon.

Surplus Value

My Michigan brother-in-law was a tool and die guy,
A machinist, fabricating parts in shops supplying Big Three
Auto makers. A bantam with thick fingers, scarred hands.
He rode a Harley soft-tail, drank Iron City, and lived
With his wife and kids in a house he mostly built himself.
During the heyday of Detroit metal, overtime and union
Contracts paid for steaks and a summer cabin
On an upstate lake and deer-season hunting trips
In the fall. He took pride in his craft and skill
Building something bigger than the Fords or Chevys
He pushed on down the line for America to drive.
Twenty years of work, good times, and happy with it.
But that road ran out. The union went south first
(Pension fraud; indictments; prison terms) and then
The companies and their money men slashed and burned
Through labor and its costs in search of market share.
The work was sweated from the men for less and less return.
Economy of scale, then of scarcity: subcontracting, piecework,
Then welfare replaced a steady pay check and bonus
Twice a year. The Harley went, the cabin; food stamps
Bought essentials, nothing more. Always quiet, he grew quieter
From day to week to month. The years that stretched ahead,
Bowing his neck, the scars grew deeper now, and inward.

During the boom that no one thought would end,
Heedless the factories flushed their waste straight into
The Saginaw River, so much so it never iced, even
In the depths of winter. Now it's frozen all year long.

Relict

My great-aunt Carlie (from Carlton, her family name)
despite Parkinson's and widow's weeds lived to be one hundred
and four years of age. Born in 1876, the Centennial year,
she passed away in 1980, living alone in the Danvers Home
for the Aged and Infirm having survived two husbands
(the first died in the 'flu epidemic of 1919, the second in 1952), sons
and daughters, assorted collateral kin, even her younger sister,
who only made it to ninety-four. Every Fourth of July
for a long time she rode in the town's Independence Day
parade, honored as Danvers' eldest citizen. A bright spark
till near the end and something of a ham, she loved waving
to the crowd from the back of a big boat Cadillac convertible,
the one with shark fins. As she aged her mind refused
to focus on the here and now. She kept a startling vision
of her father's sad decline from wealth to trade:
a turn-of-the-century decision to back kerosene,
not gasoline. A not unfamiliar history, status thereafter derived
not from money or striving but from lineage: a family,
its place in time. Avid for genealogy she traced her line –
Putnams mostly – back to the Bay Colony, the Covenant,
the City on a Hill and whatever history could be spun
from those first things. A teleology of grace and consolation
as the world passed the North Shore by. Her family – mine too –
had a window in Fanueil Hall, graves in the Old Granary,
were Patriots, fought in one or another revolutionary battle
(the details always somewhat imprecise) and formed
the backbone of the DAR and Cincinnati, those *memento
mori*s of a declining race. She never moved far from
those little towns, satellite to Boston's hub, sitting still
and calm as time washed in from somewhere else and left
her looking back, with a clearer sense of where it was she'd been.

Material Culture

Wood breathes in but gives us nothing back
For all the years since someone made it into
Something else: a shape, a form, a purposed
Work of art that a family – in this case mine –
Bought and kept since it was made some time
In the 1750s north of Boston. Danvers or Salem
Craftsmen, anonymous skillful men,
Took burled walnut, fit it to the tongue and groove
Of customary pattern, added brass fittings,
Set it out to catch the eye.
A slant front Chippendale, a desk just luxe enough
To signify a rising man but serious for the work at hand:
Merchant, lawyer, office holder. It's not known who
Bought it first. Family legend pridefully maintains
General Israel Putnam – 'Old Put' – who fought
With Washington, owned it once. A faded paper
Says so, so perhaps. But if its genealogy is intact
Albeit inexact, I want to know what it absorbed
In my family's travels from there and then to here and now:
Wood stands mute, breathing nothing back.

Aces and Eights

Early mornings, two or three a.m., when my father couldn't sleep
He'd make his way downstairs and brew a coffee, black and bitter.
Sit at the kitchen table with a pack of Luckies, a deck of cards,
Dealing out dummy poker hands, playing them himself
                                        against himself.
Five- or seven-card stud were his games; never draw, a game
                                        for kids,
He'd say, not a real man's game. Calculating odds and chances
                                    in his head,
He'd check and raise, hold and fold, spinning cards out
                                    in semicircles
To put them through their paces. Smoking all the while
                                    and sipping
From his cup, he'd impose his pattern on their random fall.
He'd learned to play, like most of the men of his generation,
                                    on football
Roadtrip bus rides and then continued in the War, breaking
                                    the monotony
Of hurry up and wait with an endless game of table stakes with cash
It was bad luck to keep, a smaller gamble of luck against
The biggest cashing out of all. Cutthroat camaraderie men learn
To relish, the poker games didn't survive once middling age,
Professional aspirations and success, domesticated affluence
(Wife; three kids) took all his time: no waiting now, all hurry.
But dealing out dummy hands was a vestigial routine, a way to fight
Another war, against daily rote, the clock, what he thought
He had become. A mindful mindlessness, the fall of pasteboard
Squares filled the night's unease, kept out the growing sense
That something had been lost someplace back in time.

*

Outside the Victorian in which we lived, the sky began to lighten.
He let the dogs out (they were his wife's), cleaned the ash tray,
                                    washed the cup,
Taking time with rituals, filling each necessary day.

Irish Graves

There's a photo somewhere
Though it's been mislaid for years:
My dad and me standing in the cemetery
Under Ben Bulben near Yeats' grave.
For a long time he was the only poet that I knew.
The tiny Kodak snapshot from early June '68
Must have been made by a caretaker
Or some other poetic tourist like ourselves.

The next day, driving back to Dublin
And the plane, we learned about the late-
Night shooting in L.A.'s Ambassador Hotel.
Instead of rain, we had sun the whole long day
And in the glare, all the Irish that we met
Looked at us and looked away in pain.

Caesura

Rain erodes – carves –
       Away a life's
Support – purpose – as sure as a
Gillette Blue Double Edge
               Cuts through essentials:
It's just a matter of time,
            Choice of weapons.

So Much for Irony

After the long night
            the false dawn reddens a low sky
      of clouds.
No summer softness

                        in the sea-brined air.

Kelp and seaweed snarl
            the tide line. Crabs scuttle, gulls swirl as tidal pools vanish
                        whirlpools to the ebb.
      Not wading I walk, bottom ooze slogging
                  grayly round my feet. Receding on the shingled beach
                  my car unlocked
                              license on the floor.

Clothes Make the Man

After my father died the chores
          of death were done
until nothing but his clothes
          remained. I stood,
my mother out walking with the dogs,
          at his closet going
through a life in cloth. From fifties'
          vanilla conformity,
demobilized khaki, academic corduroy,
          an ascending arc
of a career, gravitas stitched out in
          suits and ties
of finer text, more subtle hues; we
          buried him in his best.
And as the cloth rippled, bespoke waves
          under my casual hands,
a flicker of greed licked out: we were at
          least I thought
same sized, why let such rich things waste?
          I admired a broadcloth
three-piece banker's stripe up against my
          chest and as I did
I caught not just my father's overt scent
          of bay rum and pomade
but a tracery of something deeper, fine-
          woven in the cloth.
I put the jacket at my face to unforewarned
          go under at the sudden
cordite stink of all his working life.
          Ambushed, I could
not breathe again until all the hangers
          swung like ruined gallows.

Inheritance

In brightness's middle
a shadow falls
            shearing garden's light
to shade.

Surprise of tears
            blurs me
back to my father's suits,
            his lost cause
            of blue and gray.

We only ever spoke
            in code, of things
until the code became our selves
            all meaning lost
            and darkness

Wrapped our tongues
            in shrouds.

The Highway System

After two years, I followed the road by rote
Up the coast to my mother's house where slowly
She was dying from choked lungs. 221 interstate
Miles as fast as I could drive, each weekend
I could get away. One early morning trip, I sped
Through parts of Maryland at ninety-five, no cops
In sight, passing little towns whose names I knew
– Skaggsville, Gunpowder Falls, Aberdeen –
Where I would never stop to rest or look around.
Pressing on the road, the drive an anodyne
For what would be there when I stopped: the pain
That could not be taken on when nothing of life
Was left but the seeing of it out. Later on, we'd sit
Late, not talking much, knowing all that was left.

Canker

Gray-black beforelight,
Goya's skalls and chavs,
all beaky and socket-eyed, humped by cloak and bag,
chivvy the KIA splayed naked,
clothes, boots and arms long looted,
out on some Spanish steppe.
Raping the dead: pliering teeth,
snipping the rare ring or locket,
turning away with a shuffled kick
to the balls or after a casual piss,
splattering a hole, once a mouth.

Christmas dawn 1999.
Amidst fluorescent dread, infarcted
by muzaked carols, piss-cutting germicides, my mother dies
and scuttling attendants rifle
through her effects, divvying
whilst her wispy corpse is swabbed and
bagged, parceled for chambering.
On complaint, Hospital shrugs
prize-winning shoulders, yawns, piles
on more forms. After all, it was really
just junk really, a watch and stuff
– a brooch, a photo frame, a wedding band
no one – not her! – will ever really miss.

In afterlight's odd forgetful hours
I tongue the empty socket in my jaw
honoring the unknown dead.

Bone Cold

Out in the December bitter churchyard
The wind is barely broken by the rocks and wall.
The offices are performed: chapped exhalations of
Hoary breath: the words are whipped away.
The eye blinks at the luminescent
Rug of astroturf arranged out of absurd
Propriety to hide the mound of fresh-turned earth
As if there were no holes to fill.

Pain pulses steadily like a vein.
What was barely to be borne inhabits you like the wind.

II

The River Refuses its Name

*On the 400th anniversary of Henry Hudson's discovery
of the Hudson River (1609)*

The river was the river's before it was ours.
Pull back and see it as it was. Reverse the flow
Of time and unpeel our landscape from the land.
Take the names and maps away: the incised grid
Of highway, road, and bridge; the connective tissue
That gives a motion to our lives. Take away the imprint
Of the names we give to place and time:
This landmark, or that battle,
This statesman or that conglomerate
From overseas. The markings that we make
In all our ceaseless commerce in the world. The walls
Of glass, the city's tunnels warrened underground,
And the restless bedlam shriek of all the dailiness
That keeps our lives afloat in what we know
As life. Modern times canyoning its heedless way
Through all our pasts and all we think we can control.
So thus the reassurance that we get from naming things
To get some fictive grip on all we think we've learned
Or know, a sense of where we've been and where we go,
The habitual views that we pass by each day
Distracting us in custom's groove and rote
From what is now and what we've never really seen.

        So start over. Think beyond ourselves
This time and all that we kept out by all our putting in.
Go back to see the river as it was before we started time.
Don't think of the river as ourselves.
Don't think of the river as our history.
Don't think of the river as anything but the river:
Cold, whole, inviolate, merciless in the integrity
Of its ceaseless mountainous riverflow.

Life's Blood

Above the river, current flows
      from dam to dam,
sheer concrete waterfalls, turbines
      linked by lines
looping from steel to steel pylon
      trees dwarfing any
evergreen. The variegation of land
      and ancient waters
transmogrified, scoured into power's
      electric grid.

Deep beneath this surface of utility
      the watercourse remains,
water under water a tumultuous passageway
      carved out by years,
aspiring toward the core. Above the cut
      on submarine embankments
old Cree hunting camps and villages drift
      vague as museum exhibits
behind the glass: tracery of life's remains.
      Bear-skull totems nailed up
to honor nature's place in man dissolve,
      falling up to fall again
downstream, ashes fueling through our mills.

Ball's Bluff

after Walt Whitman

Guidon flags unfurled, snapped by the breeze
      The cavalry steps off into the ford
Splashing shallow water, sliding on river
      Rocks and moss, moving implacably
Toward a bluff beyond. Infantry follow
      Shaken out in a skirmish line, rifles
At port arms, bayonets dull steel
      In the sun-struck air.

      High ground across the stream
Dug-in rebel troops hold their breath, rifles
      Cocked and locked, zeroed on
The blue advancing line. Silence.
      Chaos then: river valley choked
With sobs, water running red.

On a landscape turned red

peach blossoms in Shiloh's bloody pond
                                  like broken bodies on the ground

Captain's Watch

By the third year of the Civil War, Whitman
Had taken to standing on Sixteenth Street
Just up from Pennsylvania Avenue, to watch
The President, solitary in his carriage, pass by
Heading north to his cottage at the Soldiers' Home
Sited on high ground, cool and distant from the
Swampy marshlands of the Executive Mansion
Whose miasma seemed to fill that house
With clouds of grief and care.

Passing each other, Lincoln in his stovepipe,
Walter (as he was known to friends but not
Posterity) in his misshapen slouch,
Would tip their hats
When they caught each other's eye.

They never spoke and never met
Even at the crowded New Year's Day open
House when the President shook the hands
Of thousands. It was Whitman's choice
To keep this distance: he feared
The furnace. Better to orbit – observing –
Than fall into that sun and be devoured.

1914

Truth be told
They were mad for it, the men
Especially, shouting streets
And squares full from Max-Joseph-Platz
To the Strand, gone wild
Like a cup final crowd
As the match-winning goal
Goes in, terraces surging
Toward the action,
A lightning bolt through bright
Blue air.

The melancholy came after,
Looking back at the time before
Emptied streets, doors hanging open
In the coal damp air.

The Magdalene Laundries

Unwanted, discarded by shame, famine,
Cold indifference of the theocratic state,
Warehoused girls perished generation
After generation, walled up in stone
Barracks – an earthly limbo of grinding
Labor for the good and great.

                Unlettered, condemned,
Desexed, forgotten, the innocents huddled
Close within cold walls. Early death came,
A mercy. Crossing over,
Bones broken, immured, scattered in forgotten
Charnel graves, their shades regathered
In another realm – graced.

Jack and Bill

Based on a true story

Between late night
And early morning, on a curb
After closing the Cedar Tavern
But still in thirst,
Pollock and de Kooning sat passing

A pint back and forth,
Trading toasts:
You're the greatest painter, Jack!
No, you're the greatest, Bill!
Until the bottle killed

The self-awareness of their own
Abstraction.

Jackson Pollock Crashes his Car

gear shift slicks
tires smoke
obscured neon
bruising the black
night light sky
reflected in oil
stained panties riding
shotgun in a Detroit lean
hard chasing stars
splashed high
above cat feet fogged
road slide-ruled plumb
through trees
rushing past to midnight's
zipper tear screams
chroming mouths
slack with idle
salt pooling lip-ward
in a gulp of wind-
ing air turned
silence spinning
wheels in chords
among desperate spheres
in ether unheard
frozen dreams westing
to zero
white canvas glaring

E.D.

Died – was carried back – the month
May –
The Pelham hills were flecked with gold –
Her garden blue – in bloom.
The town went on
Unnoticing
Its business to be done –
Her life-long work – scribbled
Scraps – audited another
World – not this one –
But rue.

Aesthetic Contemplation

The river merchant's widow (supercargo, typhoon)
Draws water from the well, yokes the buckets
On her back and bends her way into her small house.

> Evening light
> And a long-legged crane
> Perches in shallows –
> Its long neck
> Ripples the still water

The river merchant's widow grimaces:
Nightly the perfect Chinese landscape poem appears
In which alone she works.

Two San Francisco Poets

Weldon Kees' Car

was found by a cop on the beat
at 2 a.m. in a park near the Golden Gate, the
doors and windows open, fog tendrils
blowing – an easy metaphor picked up
by literary detectives trying to fathom
Kees's unexplained vanishing.
The law assumed suicide or 'death by misadventure',
empty car plus proximity to the bridge
told a familiar story. Case closed.
No body was ever found. Years later
a journalist claimed to have seen Kees somewhere down
in Mexico – probably in the same town where JFK
hangs out with Marilyn and Elvis (slim again) plays
hillbilly guitar. The reporter said Kees ducked him
having disavowed all knowledge of the arts.
Other sightings have been made, all unconfirmed.
Weldon Kees: painter, poet, specter,
Might have been. When he got lost he had
A growing reputation. He desired none.

Jack Spicer

kept a bottle always handy to drown
the words that incessantly streamed
through him like the jolt from an electric chair.
A student of linguistic theory, he concocted
a theory – incomplete, unprovable, disparaged –
that we are radio receivers for language
beamed in from somewhere else. A passive
antenna, he tried to order the chaotic words
streaming through his appalled mind,
a fizzing overload that froze his will.
Gripped by a logos he could not comprehend,
he gibbered, spoke ecstatically. People recoiled.
Tortured for years, at last he finally flipped the switch,
drank himself to death, but first diagnosed himself
precisely: 'My vocabulary did this to me.'

Nighthawks

It's late night, the couple
Must be bitterly arguing
Under their breath, picking at their
Regrets.

It's late night, the single man
Must be a robber waiting
For the couple to leave, to pull
The heist.

It's late night, the counterman
Must be a writer, thinking
About his sheaf of poems
A la Rimbaud.

It's late night, the tableau
Must be chance, meaning,
Lit by neon,
Only itself.

For Elizabeth Bishop

I caught a tremendous fish
Some big pike or lunker lake trout
And after a brief fight its resistance,
Sharp and angry, snapped the line.
It vanished. Of course what vanished
Was the thought of the fish, not the fish
Itself. I never had a chance to see it
Close: water cascading from its scales
And fins, gasping, as I boated and hefted it
Before slipping it back into
The cold lake water of upstate Maine.
Losing the tension of the line, the canoe
Rocked in recoil; the wind
Came up and turned the water into chop.
I headed in with the story of my catch
To tell the others all about.

My parents went to a rare reading
Bishop promised at Harvard in '79.
When it was announced that she had died
That afternoon, the shocked hush was broken
By all the poets in the crowd getting up
And reading from her work, holding up
Those gorgeous fish for all to hear about.

Camouflage Self-Portrait

In 1987, at fifty-nine, Andy Warhol,
played out from the modern life he made
(after the first lunch with Jackie O / there is no other)
faked his own death – routine gallbladder procedure:
gone awry – slipped quietly from the hospital
back into his mother's house, his Pittsburgh boyhood
home. Wig gone, black suit and fancy glasses trashed, he
donned the clothes and life of a nondescript working man,
took a bakery assistant's job making crullers
and cakes, introduced himself as Stosh from somewhere
vaguely somewhere else, joined the local bowling league.
He learned to polka at the Legion Hall, amiably fending off
the local widows, and grew quietly old alone.
He cooked for one and after dinner sat and watched
the neighborhood wind down from dusk to night.
He developed a real fondness for baseball:
it was so slow.

Itch

On a photograph by Satomi Shirai

Queens bridge rumble
Train, backwash of silence
Caught now in evening light
– Apartment clutter, warm like
I like it, like life, and as I like it:
On my terms, alone or with
Another, passing through or
Staying on, but on my terms
Inviolate to any whim of others
Or of the world itself. My time
Alone, the whole world open
To my devising light and all
It brings, creating my present,
My past. My art itches:
I scratch it into life.

Adulthood

Optimistic to think that contentment lies
just around the corner like a dozy cat.
That with middle age a mellow fruitfulness
will appear by right, right as expected.
Gratefully you'll welcome it in to suffuse
your gaze, your entire aspect, with benignity:
acceptance in all its facets, all becoming all.

Foolish to think that contentment strays
anywhere near the neighborhood. Instead with middle
age a ratcheting sense of slippage, a scrabbling on
the climb just trying to keep your shirt tucked in.
Resigned never to attain cruising speed, your gaze
cold as a gun. How little there is all in all.

Federal City Scenes

Noon

Bureaucrats washing out of offices at lunch time into
The brief meridian of the downtown street. Sunlight
Shearing across and down, drawn die-straight by the
Tops of office blocks: marking the noontime transit
Of an accelerated hour – as if time were not a constant
Measure – of short respite before the tide ebbs back again.

Plumage

This season's fashion in ties has shifted to floral red
Splashes after pausing briefly in yellow with a segue into repp:
Stylish but never too outré, the young men (up and comers!)
Stay just behind the edge of the curve. As they always do.

Alexander Wept

The petty tyrannies of daily life at office jobs:
Bureaucratic worlds to conquer. Empires are small now.

Myriads of Eternity

Two-deckers backed against thruways and rail freight
Shunting yards; cars go by all day. The light
Stanchions of the old ball park crane above the flat
Roof line after line of brick row houses. Meanly portioned
Backyard spaces done up as best one can: grass and garden plots,
Flowers bend to the chemical gauze filtering yellow light.
Front door stoops, two concrete slab steps whitewashed yearly,
Soap-scrubbed weekly against the bellying smokestack clouds.

At street corner bus stops, 5 a.m. men with broken feet,
Cracked hands, stiff in coveralls, waiting for the day to start.
The arriving buses carry back the women who work
Downtown at night in office blocks. The buses
Used to run all day, now they barely run at all.
Work's will is done.

For those who hear what we cannot

The madman, skirled at dusk by a late
    autumn wind, sits cricked on a stone bench
Knee balancing a typewriter in his mind.
      An old Royal beater perched on the pullout ledge
Of a yard sale, varnished study desk
    in a cone of lambent yellow suspended
Alongside shelves and stacks of file-cards folders
    notebooks teetering with accreted ordered
Marshalled facts. Material bulked to fill out others' pasts
    and his present lives,
Establishing order his own fragile self cannot maintain.
    Fallen now through the study's floor
Into the strange angled November light
    he hunches, hammering down each fictive page
Elbows beating like a diving seabird's wings
    Thrashing away at darkness. Into light.

Saints Today

The frame
of poverty,
cracked paint and
water marked.
Wreckage.
The good
intentions
gone awry
beaten like a
rug you lie
bewildered by
the size
of what's beyond
your door.
Receding fast, life
leaks
away
like tears of blood
from daily
arrows.

Internal Difference

The air thick with years of chalk motes
Acrid, cutting the damp wool fug from winter coats
Pegged in a line along one wall. Schoolchildren
Serried in old-fashioned seats and fliptop desks
Bow to their teacher or to something anyway.
Among them an ordinary boy quiet in chain-store
Corduroy: a nondescript, adrift in more than lessons.
The taste of sour milk fills his mouth.

No schoolchildren triggered reveries then
In the graying hour before the alarm.
Forty years on in my eye's mind I double back
Into and outside myself, at once familiar and
A distant other. Impossible to – yet impossible
Not to wish to – retrieve the intervening time
Rising once before my own small distant figure.

The clock trips over, begins its electronic rasp,
As if time were starting up again.

Permanent Record

Plangent, a youthful haze goldens the boomer tract
House cul-de-sac on a California summer's eve. Children skirl.
Then, a derisory whistle and 'Let's see that one again':
The one-armed man, his scar-pink stump a sideshow act
Peeping from a white tee sleeve, as with a careless whirl
My bike tangles, skidding me from skylarking into pain.

Lolling by his car's raised hood, tuning fuel injection,
Pompadour slicked back high racy, a tough pre-Beatle
Coxcomb to match egos with his wound. Snake and eagle
Twining down that absent arm to a fist clenched at Choisin.

Adults give off distance and weight imposing
To make a child snuffle more than any pavement's rasp.
But as the arc of my tear-rimmed glare flicked past
His grin, I caught the tangled inner wound, self-hate.
Linked, I was the past for him. His was my fate.

Teleology

Wouldn't everything have been a lot easier
      if: Arriving at the terminal
the lovers missed each other, and wandered
      aimless in the crowds until,
one waiting in the bar, the other leafing magazines,
      they both picked up casual
conversations with strangers which quickly moved
      with an audible click,
brushing a lock of hair, having a second drink,
      to something else, from which
brush contact they both danced slowly and then
      suddenly into long loves full
of children and delight. Thus forestalling the
      inevitable slow slough of boredom
and middle-class routine – ennui with adultery,
      outbreaks of broken crockery –
for which a dyspeptic not too attentive God marked them.
      So that years later both
tried to recall who it was they were to meet that day but
      gave up with a laugh
after a thought's flicker to make dinner and love.

Instead, time unrolled for them as for empires:
      drawn through the crowd ineluctably
they met and in a second fell.

Hypocrite lecteur. Whose *semblable?*

I work all day and make sure no one sees me
Drunk at night. I keep hidden even from myself
Cupboarded out of sight against the inspectors who come round
To spot-check you up from time to time.

But when on their regular rounds they knock
I make myself ready at the door: shined shoes and teeth
Beaming in my blue success suit, my spiel wound up, set to go.
With shoulders squared I send my Potemkin self out on parade:

My dog, two kids, this lovely house and wife:
 These are the wellsprings of my creative life.
Neuroses, problems, angst or mess? No. Alienated?
  Never. I'm not just 'just all right': I'm centered
In all senses. Actualized, complete, self-realized.
  My urine like my mind is clear. I love all peoples.
My parents too. I sign petitions for worthy causes.

Left, right, left: I swing along to the music they expect to hear
Until smiling I'm checked off to shuffle back
Into the priest hole of my life and, in my mind's ear only, howl.
The darkness is not just soundless now: it's not even dark.

Hemingway's Iceberg

I sit at my desk, writing an essay,
'The Amputated Self: The Masculine Voice in Modern
American Poetry',
about how men make a virtue
from necessity. The codes
which hide men from themselves. Their self-denying ordinances
of speech not speech.
Hit by a pitch, the batter
never rubs the spot, trots to first. 'Come back,
Shane!' But riding away, a man's gotta do what a man's
gotta do. The belief in things.
The idiot idea
that what's not there, what can't be expressed, is there
by its denial, its exclusion. The sacred heart
of unacknowledged wounds,
ignored until it can't be hidden.

Under the green
slosh of waves, implacable dark
seeps coldly up through bone
to brain and you're alone.

Isn't it pretty to think so?

Fathers playing catch
with sons:
American as wheatfields mown
into ball fields around which
great cities are built and on which
a golden light still congregates undimmed.

This father
playing catch with
this son: a stinging rebuke
sizzles in over
and over again, stitches thrumming
redly, welting a child's palm
through arm to blood-fogged brain.
Pitching with intent: 'Come on!
Be a Man!'

I want to learn
and not be told and then have
that telling gilded
in a myth which smothers
our unease
at beaten fathers beating sons.

Jamais Vu or Was It?

Seductive is the easy elegy
to the way things never were.
This porch, that swing,
a kid's first crush, buzz of bees.
At dusk, parabolas of skipping ropes,
a baseball looped from a boy's arm
to dad's hand. Deep in chairs, adults murmur
what adults murmur at day's end.
Always, a melancholy sense of something
coming on that never quite arrives.
Life becoming the apprehension
of all its ordinary beauty, a kaleidoscope
with no surprises in the resolution of
shape and form at each day's shaking.

That's not the way it was, you say.
And you are, of course, exactly right.
Dad got bitter after a drink or three
and muttered about missed chances.
Mother cried unnervingly at sudden times.
The Russians stole the Bomb and Emmett
Till got lynched. That girl never
liked me after all and the grass was
always patchy brown by June.

Except that was exactly how we think it
was. The past is how we've learned to face
each day's tidal pull. We stitch the pattern
up around our selves. It fits,
a second skin. What should have been
becomes what was, what is. Our lives
become a facing to structure selves
so chancy and so frail, one look's
honest touch would break them into
desire's hopeless shards. History
isn't written by the victors but by
the victims, day after every day.

Still Life, Grand Central Station

Buy the premise and you buy the drink,
the glittering bottled landscape of
your dreams. Set-ups – setting out –
shiny and bright rainbow of glass and ice
– olives and pearl onions – swank the bar
as westward the course of empire takes your sway.
Just one quick pop before the train,
its bullet blows right through you,
stains your shirt with what is beyond,
the shards and shards of presque-vue.
The what of what has almost been. Doubled,
in the mirror something flicks, a trout across
a too-clear pool: too quick to grasp except
in recognition that it's past. You almost held
it once but now it's down to white nights and TV,
the finality of women's heels, hissing phones.
Office walls are gray to match your fate,
the calendar unchanging, time in spate.

Alcools

Remember the flaring
manic nights, the crackle
riding shotgun into dawn.
The quiet first sip in the still lit bar
or the first one of the day: the
necessary glow of glass.

Not the after wreck. Time and future
all holed out. The disappeared:
this job, those friends, a family
somewhere else. Not the spittle
flecks and the snake's tongue
flicking out.

Marginalia

Presto! the cabinet flourishes,
the bikini babe jumps out restored, no longer sliced in two.
Sleight of hand works
only for other people who effortlessly pluck
the ace from a bloom of doves. In your case, feet
metastasize, bulging your swaybacked boots like hydroponic
artichokes. Collars tightening
with each day's alarum, grindstones roughen to a dull nub
no oil can smooth. Years.
Meanwhile, success is for someone else who
yet against the forensics sees himself as on a edge,
arms flailing, a fat man wandering on thinning ice, wondering
how the milk got on *your* whiskers.

Call Waiting. Waiting...

Exurban lawns, green slick with grass
emollients. Computer plantings. A blow-in from the Arctic turns,
bemused, heading out, with nicitating eyes.
Barbecue grills, chefs with funny hats
and aprons (assembly lined, is a joke a joke?), briquet a
darkness, scrumbling the dusk's light.
No election news fizzes in
through the ether as hearts go south. No surfing here. Wood
and brick click, the invisible tick of atom clocks notching
the changes until the stirrup snaps, extinguishing close
hearing, small sounds. And then animals run
across thinning slates roofing detached
houses. Their thrumming paws
rip like Ringo on a roll. Adulteries, arranged by phone
kept by rote, mechanical, a groove
of 4/4 time. Regular as the news.

Not Enough Room to Swing a Cat

As insomniac curtains billow, the certainty
that local knowledge is always wrong: that dowsing
by the old mill wall fonts no springs to flower
a fruited plain of jars.
That that whittler on the porch will always
send you a way so wrong it's almost right until the end
when ambush rattles
choke-mouthed through the fonds. Dry-mouthed
prairies roll away to post-office murals painted by the yard
of hardpack with a statue to the pioneers, or something like
                                        them anyway.
Who wants to think what life is really like?
Better to follow the curtain's flourish up and out beyond
to where mountains shout and July snow promises above trees.
Mystic to the end, the road hangs heavy toward the horizon,
heading south. Or is it east? Anywhere so long
as out of Dodge and its entangling appliances.
Fuchsia is the wedding color but next year black
will be back in style, reversed boots.

Summer Vacation

So what happened there? And when? Seems familiar
Yet different too. Out of nowhere the flowers disappeared,
Clouds cut to the chase, horizons glowed, the aftershocks
Were felt for years. Photographs curled and browned: sepia
Worlds. The scent of road-smoke lingered
For years. Enough already! Time to make a plan –
A schedule. That's the ticket. Requiring verve,
A sense of purpose to get from here to there and back again

Without interruptions or distress. A cooling drink
Would be just right, an aperitif with ice to go with foreign vistas
Or the old familiar. Just make sure you bring enough
For everyone to share. Respect the customs of the house.
Remember to tip your hat to stray dogs on the street.
Leave your book at home, take a walk, see what you meet.

The Sublime Meets Prairie Town

Rain stops down the street
signals left and rolls
on, sheeting the town
from stem to stern, obscuring
the air with the false
promise of thunderheads
and change. Squalls don't
shift the shape of things
long enough to matter.
All style, sublime foreboding
never delivers its electric
promise.
       Quickly, sugar beet
fields, water towers, angle-
parked trucks outside main-street
stores, luncheon counters
and threshers starting up again
re-emerge from rain's distancing
sepia. Clouds roll away,
uncovering the constant line
of space and plain.
The horizon glares
her eye as the storm winks out
its promise. She runs the laundry out
again across the drying yard. Sheets
billow. The line pulleys out, endlessly
returns to her constant hand.

III

Zero Sum

Last visit:
>   Phoned through
>   Protective screen
Last appeal:
>   No recourse
>   5–4 against
Last meal:
>   One olive
>   One pit
Last walk:
>   Manacled shuffle
>   Tie-Down squad
Last rites:
>   'Father forgive me…'
>   'Father forgive them…'
Last act:
>   Death warrant
>   Color of law
Last words:
>   'I'm…'
>   'You're…'
Last sight:
>   Cold halo
>   White light
Last breath:
>   Choked
>   Out
Last lesson:
>   Death penalty
>   Kills us

Anti-Hymn/Antonym: A Prophecy

Take me to the river
Wash me in the water. Let me dream
The dream to hope again
And then I fail instead...

Fallen from high distance
Scattered through far fields,
Encase me now in asphalt
Douse me down in flame

Anneal the world of loss with pain
And buildings built of dread.
Stop up the river
Of all hearts. And
Disregard the dead.

At 9:45 a.m.

on 9/11, as we know it now,
Gene Smith, coming back from the dentist, walks up
subway stairs, out into the skirling dust of History.

Thinking of his family, calculating, he turns with the crowd,
walks north to the Terminal
and gets on the first bus heading out.

One year later, on the dot, Gene Smith, in short sleeves
and a careful smile, walks to work
in the town of M___, state of I___.

Back in Bayside, his widow, hollowed by the
mourning rote, touches their son's hand to the
graven name and years: closure of a sort.

Unintended Consequences

Did lightness
or brightness fall
from the air? Opinions differed.
Yet amid bombast, something changed
without our knowing quite what,
or how it happened. Suddenly,
overnight, everything
went slightly out of kilter. Foundations
shifted, maps no longer fit
the landscape. Familiar verities
disappeared, popped up again
in far-off places, hallways disarranged.
Night came on so early,
dawn was always later:
after a while it never arrived at all.

Colossus

He knew what he knew
and did not know
what he did not know
which was
America.

The city
The hill
The river:
all a blank
in his one-eyed mind.

His voice silted
the city's streets
flattened the hill
stilled the river flow
to his gray resolve.

The bread
no longer the body.
The wine
no longer the body.
The body

no longer the body.
The horn's bell
mute, full of dry
and bitter
fruit.

He knew what he knew
and did not know
what he knew
was not
America.

CCTV

From my mother's sleep I fell into the State.
                                    – Randall Jarrell

You're watching me sleep
While I sleep. You're watching
My tits while I sleep. You're
Watching an internet monitor
While I sleep. You're bored
Watching my bedroom
While I sleep. You're hoping
Something will happen while
I sleep. Something to break
The white nights while I sleep.
Maybe you're wanking or having
A coffee while I sleep. Maybe
You're not even there
                    While I sleep.
But the cameras are always on
And you'll sleep soon now too –
The day shift coming in, monitoring
An empty bed. The Government
Is always keeping watch to always
Keep us safe as houses
                    While we sleep.

Death from Above

GameBoy is a model modern fighter jock:
Rocks RayBans and a Corvette Z,
Pumps steel in the health club gym
To trim his swagger high and tight
And keep his dick slick for the hot chix
Who hang around the hot tub bar and pool
Flaunt thongs and beestung lips
For warrior heroes on a mission
To do God and Nation proud.

Far away, in icy black near-space
A satellite rotates its panoptic eye
And hunts. Calibrating, its electronic ears
Prick up: spots a crowd on the road
Where no crowds are allowed to be.
Back down in his air-conditioned bunker
– Base Zero, California; Condition Black –
GameBoy flips his toggle over, drives the drone
To blow an Afghani wedding straight to hell.

Def: Extreme Rendition

Rendition 'The handing over of a fugitive
Or some other party
Of interest to the duly constituted
Authority of the State
Or its representative.'

Rendition A surrender; a submission:
A bringing –
To the knees.
A bagging of the head
And eyes – the state
Of nullity.

Rendition Sing me the song
That's why you're here
Give me the stuff
We want to hear.
Spiel me the tune boy
And you might
Stay OK but you know
What happens
If you don't want to play.

Render Tear skin from flesh
Break bone
Break
And boil, reduce to grease.
Reheat. Repeat
As necessary and desired.

Render Unto Caesar –
Or eat the thorns –

Render End Here. Enter Here.

The End of History

The worn knife, sharpened to a mercy,
Poised tight on the son's jugular,
The neck offered, right knee pushing
The boy's back, left hand cupping
The boy's eyes, pulling back
Against the knee braced in the
Boy's back. Eternal pose.

Sun sliding down, time starts:
The father's eyes fill with salt
The boy pisses himself
The knife slips
Slicing a shark red wake
Splashing the naked rock.

Where is the Angel now?

Acknowledgements and Notes

I would like to thank Michael Schmidt and Helen Tookey, my editors at Carcanet, for their moral and editorial support of this volume. I'd also like to acknowledge the editors of the journals in which many of these poems appeared for the first time. Finally, the authorial cliché 'words cannot express' nonetheless expresses my feelings for my brothers Chris and Andrew: thanks fellas!

'June, Swoon' was written for Brooklyn artist Elizabeth Huey's 2009 Lunar Festival. The title comes from the old Tin Pan Alley ditty about rhymes and songwriting: 'moon, June, swoon'.

'Ball's Bluff': the short, violent Civil War battle of Ball's Bluff occurred on 21 October 1861. A disorganised and ill-planned Union assault across a ford in the Potomac River and up a steep bluff was repulsed with heavy casualties: 223 killed, 226 wounded, 553 captured. Confederate casualties totalled about 150. The debacle caused consternation and controversy in the North.

'On a landscape turned red': the battle of Shiloh was fought on 6 and 7 April 1862. It was a narrow Union victory as the Confederates broke off first, both sides exhausted after two days of combat on a battlefield roughly four miles square. Combined casualties numbered 25,000. The battle began on Easter Sunday and is named after Shiloh Church, a Methodist meeting house.

'The Magdalene Laundries' concerns the ongoing scandal in Ireland of the treatment of unwed mothers who were cast out from society, institutionalised and forced to live as virtual slave labour for the Church and State. The scandal involves both the policy itself – a modern horror – and the subsequent cover-up and denial by various officialdoms of what had occurred.

'Itch' was written in response to a photograph of the same title by the artist Satomi Shirai. Her *Itch* was included in *Asian American Portraits of Encounter*, National Portrait Gallery, Washington, DC, 2011–12. It can be found at www.npg.si.edu and at www.satomishirai.com.

'Zero Sum': this poem on the death penalty was immediately inspired by the 'last meal' project of photographer Helen Grace

Ventura Thompson, particularly her striking 'portrait' of the single olive requested by Victor Feguer, executed in Iowa in 1963; the olive's pit was found in Feguer's suit after he was hanged. Thompson's photograph is the cover image for this book.

'Colossus' became part of a collaboration with Washington, DC artist Nekisha Durrett that she created at the Hillyer Art Space, Washington, DC, 2008–09.

'Death from Above' was part of a collaboration with English artist Scarlet Monahan.

Many of these poems first appeared in my pamphlet, *Internal Difference* (Lintott/Carcanet, 2011).

'Still we pretend at modesty', 'No Place', 'Surplus Value', 'Relict', 'Material Culture', 'Aces and Eights', 'On a landscape turned red', 'Two San Francisco Poets', 'Colossus', '*Def*: Extreme Rendition' and 'The End of History' first appeared in *PN Review*. These poems were also included in *New Poetries V: An Anthology*, edited by Michael Schmidt with Eleanor Crawforth (Carcanet, 2011), along with 'The River Refuses its Name' and 'Teleology'.

'Jackson Pollock Crashes His Car', 'The Sublime Meets Prairie Town', 'Slake', '*Alcools*', 'At 9:45 a.m.', 'The River Refuses its Name', '*Hypocrite lecteur. Whose semblable?*', '*Jamais Vu* or Was It?' and 'June, Swoon' first appeared in *Illuminations* (College of Charleston, South Carolina).

'Not Enough Room to Swing a Cat', 'Still Life, Grand Central Station', 'Saints Today', 'Adulthood' and 'Clothes Make the Man' first appeared in *Poem* (University of Alabama, Huntsville).

'Anti-Hymn/Antonym: A Prophecy' first appeared in *The Battersea Review*.

'Internal Difference' first appeared in *Potomac Review*.

'Itch' first appeared in *Insight Photographs*.

'For those who hear what we cannot' first appeared in *Talking River Review*.

'Isn't it pretty to think so?' first appeared in *Aethlon: The Journal of Sport Literature*.